Also by Devin Johnston

POETRY

Mosses and Lichens ∗ *Far-Fetched* ∗ *Traveler*
Sources ∗ *Aversions* ∗ *Telepathy*

PROSE

Creaturely and Other Essays ∗ *Precipitations*

CONTENTS

Dragons * 3

Mist * 5

Monody * 7

Elegy for a Hen * 10

Morning Glory * 12

After Wyatt * 14

Georgia Blizzard * 16

Fourteen * 18

From a Notebook * 19

Common Yarrow * 23

The Fox * 24

The First Troubadour * 25

New France * 27

Last Song * 29

Unexpected Guests * 31

Another April * 38

The Leash * 40

At Fifty: A Letter * 44

At Ninety-Two * 48

A Toast * 50

Futilities * 51

Prufrock * 54

Living Dead * 57

Beulah Land * 59

Lingering in Alabama * 61

Little Egypt * 63

Chester, Illinois * 65

Bière de Garde * 67

Notes from a Campaign * 69

Kudzu * 71

A Bat in Daylight * 73

Cold Trail * 74

Fifteen * 75

Tributary * 76

Landfall * 77

Kea * 79

Tui * 80

The Marlborough Sounds * 81

Acknowledgments * 85

DRAGONS

DRAGONS

DEVIN JOHNSTON

Farrar Straus Giroux * New York

RAGONS

Farrar, Straus and Giroux
120 Broadway, New York 10271

Library of Congress Control Number: 2022949037
ISBN: 978-0-374-60730-2

Designed by Crisis

Our books may be purchased in bulk for promotional, educational,
or business use. Please contact your local bookseller or the
Macmillan Corporate and Premium Sales Department at 1-800-221-7945,
extension 5442, or by email at MacmillanSpecialMarkets@macmillan.com.

www.fsgbooks.com
www.twitter.com/fsgbooks
www.facebook.com/fsgbooks

1 3 5 7 9 10 8 6 4 2

There are groans and growls, dun clouds and sunshine mixed in a huge phantasmagoria that never rests, never ceases to unfold into—the day's poor little happenings.

WILLIAM CARLOS WILLIAMS, *Kora in Hell*

DRAGONS

We gathered in a field southwest of town,
several hundred hauling coolers
and folding chairs along a gravel road
dry in August, two ruts of soft dust
that soaked into our clothes
and rose in plumes behind us.

By noon we could discern their massive coils
emerging from a bale of cloud,
scales scattering crescent dapples
through walnut fronds,
the light polarized, each leaf tip in focus.

As their bodies blotted out the sun,
the forest faded to silverpoint.
A current of cool air
extended from the bottomlands
an intimation of October,
and the bowl of sky deepened
its celestial archaeology.

Their tails, like banners of a vast army,
swept past Orion and his retinue
to sighs and scattered applause,
the faint wail of a child crying.
In half an hour they had passed on
in search of deep waters.

Before our company dispersed,
dust whirling in the wind,
we planned to meet again in seven years
for the next known migration.
Sunlight flashed on windshields

and caught along the riverbank
a cloudy, keeled scale
about the size of a dinner plate,
cool as blanc de Chine
in the heat of the afternoon.

MIST

Around a bend, the wide Missouri
rises to erase itself,
blank beyond a beaded rail,
where muted masses loom and melt
to kaolin's soft nothingness.
From the river bottom, a grand staircase
cut from calcite limestone
and built by the WPA
climbs through sycamores and cloud,
a ziggurat of flights and landings
leading nowhere,
a path of lost intention
or reef of the imagination
calcified, the stone itself
once the bed of ocean life.
Some speak of a paranormal
red mist on the stairs at dusk,
perhaps the powdered ghost
of Paleozoic crinoids
or ocher of the Sac and Foxes'

unrecorded rites.

A stone's throw from the topmost tread

bindweed has obscured

a K-9 cemetery

where urns of German shepherds

go untended,

the last Max forgotten.

Sunset warms the somber bricks

of Bellefontaine Habilitation,

each unit broken down

into numbered "homes."

What does it mean to have a home?

One resident attempts to feed

her nightgown through a jammed shredder.

Another, mostly blind, rocks

back and forth in agitation

before a muted television

across which shadows flit

haphazardly through river mist,

renouncing any path.

MONODY

When you wake
a shaft of sunlight
undulates
through ancient glass
with the heft and timbre
of *cor de nuit*
to glow on gray paint.

Again at dusk
an unstopped beam
shines through plants
and kitchen blinds
with the same soft timbre
and sustain,

a calm plaint
through scattered cloud
mornings and evenings,
rising and setting,
the same yet different,
different yet the same.

Organ stops
speak no names,
only tones,
the resonance
of pressured air
that flows through ranks
as through your days,

feeling implied
through pliant rhythms,
harmonics heard
but not engraved.

While you sleep
a whippoorwill
pipes unseen
through ranks of reeds
whip-poor-will
whip-poor-will
with the wobble of
a spinning wheel,

the lightest friction
that repeats
only itself

unendingly,
each time around
the same yet different,
different yet the same.

ELEGY FOR A HEN

For ten springs you circled the yard
in step beside your sister,
in league with stones of the field
through all kinds of weather,
basking in August heat,
high-stepping through snow,
or charging squirrels through wild
carrot and common yarrow,
white wings outstretched
in raptorial threat.
Feathers without flight
kept the world withdrawn,
whatever came and went,
no politics beyond
the flock's nesting box
or the shadow of a Cooper's hawk
across the coop and run.
For ten springs, dusk and dawn,
the days linked so lightly,
until a soft morning in March:

the dull glint of glazed metals,
chimney pots and rooftops gray,
nothing between them and the gray
rain clouds settling down,
your body nothing but a bundle
of feathers and featherlight bones.

MORNING GLORY

Why call this plant a weed? Some flowers
evince no difference between
giving and taking, all their powers
dispersed unseen beyond a stile
that your wants might for a little while
be mine, and open to the light.

Some flowers don't care where they grow,
climbing and trailing across the bricks
with no trellis of metaphysics
or narrow bed to call their own,
careless as a worm through wood.
Quiebra platos, breaker of plates!
Their tendrils overwhelm the slates
of copingstones that have withstood
sleet and snow, the ragged comb
in late September hid below
a crest of papyraceous foam.

Tough and tissue soft, loose blossoms
open for a while to sense,
whatever slant of daylight comes,
then close to cold in a slow wince.

AFTER WYATT

They slip away, those creatures who
once caught my eye and ventured near,
near enough to smell of snow
as cold lingered in their fur
and breath warmed my sleeping ear;
who ate an apple from my hand
and lounged in sunlight, unconstrained.

Such old affections slip away,
all but one, *la douce dolor*:
she leaned above me as I lay
stretched out on the kitchen floor,
caught within her net of hair;
then quickened by a passing mood,
she softly asked, *Does that feel good?*

She lingered in my consciousness
when I awoke, a bit confused
to find her gone, the place a mess,

and emptiness come home to roost.
I wonder if she'd be amused
to see me settled down, and if
she still pursues that wayward life.

GEORGIA BLIZZARD

Some dark November morning
when troubles circle round,
go quarry clay from Plum Creek
and bring it home in a tow sack,
a blue-gray lump still cold enough
to make your fingers ache.

Mix it with a filler of sand
and flux of silky ash,
then shape an urn of earthenware
about the size of a salt-pig
with a human face
and panther haunches.

When foes distress your waking mind,
and clay turns hard as leather,
burnish the urn with sassafras,
a tonic for protection.
Low fire in a steel drum

and flash the flanks to russet.
Get rid of taunting things
by bringing them to the surface.

Once the urn has cooled and sits
pinging faintly on a bench,
blow across its lip
to resonate a low tone,
as when the wind moans through a gap,
Who will weep for Edith?

Come what may, the pot will hold
no phlox, no ashes, nothing but
the hollow shape of thought.

FOURTEEN

By fourteen, the heart turns strange, mercurial in mood:
the flash of silver dulls to lead, now indolent, now rude.

You who sought me out for help now shut the bedroom door,
a voluntary quarantine from all that you abhor.

You shut the blinds against the sun, against the trees in bloom,
and test a gift you gave yourself, a bottle of perfume.

Indole, a fragrant molecule in flowers and in feces,
attracts the curiosity of pollinating bees:

it smells of jasmine on the vine, or jasmine's counterfeit
dispersed in the evening air, and yet, it smells of shit in shit.

What would it smell like by itself? Like ink from iron gall,
a cake of Chinese indigo, or some damp animal.

A pungent odor, dark yet brisk. Sequestered in your room,
you text or scribble furtively to concentrate the gloom.

FROM A NOTEBOOK

With the Tick Tock
dark and locked,

swing and slide
taped off,

families turn
in on themselves.

See you on the other side.

*

The pullout trash bin
in the kitchen

slowly trundles open
unbidden,

soft thunder
at 3 a.m.

Covers pull away
on an ebbing tide.

*

The city entertains no plans
this somber holiday,
only vestiges of play,
the clash of pots and pans,
rough music in lieu of pay.
Timor mortis conturbat me.

*

Warmed by sunlight
books ripen
on the windowsill,

lignin
of yellow paper
releasing the aroma
of vanillin,

the atmosphere
of *Sentimental
Education.*

*

Pale flowers,
prickles of desire,
snowflakes
on a spring morning

as the sun returns
to Svalbard,
*where people are
neither born nor buried.*

*

Black crepe streamers.
The sad dignity of entranceways
to turn-of-the-century houses
built before vaccines.
In one window
a curtain lifts and drops.
Somewhere deep inside
someone prods a piano.

*

In the park
only couples
stroll close together
through sunlit fields,
clarified dyads,
while an old man
shuffles his walker
along a shaded path,
head within
a cardboard box
in which he's cut
the eye slit
of a great helm.

COMMON YARROW

In hard times, across bewildered lawns:
A weed to staunch the wounds of Myrmidons.

THE FOX

A fourth-grader sees the fox
skulking behind the Climatron
as something from the rural past,
Reynard, the sly antagonist
of Chanticleer and gingerbread,
ghostly tip of tail for wit,
fur waistcoat immaculate.

But foxery is futurist,
a whiff of what's upwind, a knack
for slipping past apocalypse.
When all intention fails, the fox—
which never had a human use—
will revel in irrelevance,
rolling in the uncut grass.

THE FIRST TROUBADOUR

Poppies bloom in ditches,
millefleur,
and sunlight fades
a tapestry
of silk and wool.

Le Puy-Notre-Dame
rings a bell,
the prolonged calling
of a name,
an open vowel.

At dusk, Jeanne d'Arc
passed this way,
and with the morning larks,
Guillaume
de Poitiers

left a bit of intimate
apparel,

the Virgin Mary's
knotted
belt or girdle,

brought back from Antioch
supposedly,
and locked within
a silver
reliquary.

Then looke who list,
sunflowers turn
their seedy heads
from east to west
to catch the sun,

ten thousand drawn
by *fin'amor* to find
a source that feeds
a fire
in the mind.

NEW FRANCE

It takes the stranger long to learn
each local mispronunciation
of names left by *coureurs de bois*.
A long way from the Tuileries
and the soft crunch of gravel walks,
Gravois rhymes with *Illinois*
at the ragged edge of Nouvelle-France,
an avenue without renewal
on which the evening sun goes down.

It may take years and years to learn
each inconvenient indirection
through parishes of Pawpaw French,
the barricades and cul-de-sacs
where children congregate at dusk,
at ease above their handlebars.

A long way from the Tuileries,
where swans patrol a standing pool
in calligraphic harmony,

you turn on Chouteau Avenue.
No stranger to desuetude,
you know each symptom of neglect,
the fence of scribbled honeyvine
or cairn of dust and gravel crushed
from the city's porous bedrock,
an aggregate of lost intent.

Far from any pied-à-terre,
the puddle left from last night's rain
reflects no cream of Paris stone,
but only *les nuages qui passent* . . .
the passing clouds, the setting sun.

LAST SONG

after Guiraut Riquier

It's for the best that I stop singing.
Songs should come from happiness,
and lately I've felt less and less
inspired, with my horizon shrinking.
When I recall my darkest days
and contemplate a world ablaze
and dread extinctions of tomorrow,
who could wonder at my sorrow?

My fire dwindled long ago.
I rake the ashes, fitting muse
for crafting esoteric blues
from scraps of what I feel and know:
at dusk, a woodcock on the wing
tumbles into early spring,
and yet in verse such things express
a feeling of belatedness.

These days, authorities dismiss
the subtle circuitries of rhyme
as relics of another time
or quaint devices that persist
on shelves of kitsch and curios.
Why not attempt a work in prose—
a memoir to mythologize
my progress through a world of lies?

We live with gaps, hypocrisies,
and flights of happiness brought low,
estranged from what we feel and know.
As every instrument agrees,
we live in seasons out of sync,
a February on the brink
of never, snow extinguishing
the first magnolia blossoming.

This dread has tainted everything:
each dawn I come to consciousness
in panic, prickles of distress,
and clench my teeth. Why would I sing?
Towhees still propose a slow
familiar tune, but no words follow;
this ache of feeling finds no phrase,
no means by which to mourn or praise.

UNEXPECTED GUESTS

after Ovid

Beneath the slopes of Sipylus—
the massif with its weeping rock—
an oak and linden have conjoined
encircled by a retaining wall,
the ring an ancient covenant
of which this story offers proof.
I've seen the place with my own eyes:
a diplomatic errand
brought me to those lands once ruled
by Tantalus, who sacrificed
his own child to outraged gods,
then spent the stagnant afterlife
sunk in a still pool,
forever tantalized by fruit
that ripens out of reach.
Not far off there lies a marsh,
once dry land, the village streets
now thronged with coots and cormorants.
Jove came there in human guise

with Mercury, who laid aside
both wand and wings. In search of rest,
they knocked on a thousand doors and found
a thousand locked, no room to let.
Just one opened hospitably,
a poor cottage thatched with reed.
Old Baucis and Old Philemon,
a kindly couple married young,
had aged together in that house
in plain and weathered poverty
they bore without complaint.
Call for master or servant there,
you'd get no answer: just those two
made up the household, and just those two
gave and followed the same command.
So when the skylords came to call
and stooped beneath the lintel stone,
the old man brought a bench on which
Baucis threw a homespun cloth.
She stirred ashes on the hearth
and stoked the embers with leaves and bark,
then blew a little to feed the flames.
She split kindling and broke up twigs
she'd kept dry, and stacked them round
a little copper cooking pot.

Whatever kale her husband could scrounge
from the kitchen garden, she washed and chopped,
and with a carving fork took down
a flitch of bacon cured with salt
from the blackened rafter where it hung
and dropped a rasher in the rolling boil.
As they passed the time in talk—
for what is time for us *but* talk?—
the couple filled a beechwood bowl
with warm water for the guests to wash.
They set a cushion stuffed with sedge
on frame and feet of willow wood
and covered it with a kilim
only brought out on holidays,
though faded now and worn enough
to suit a well-worn life.
The gods sat down. Aproned, Baucis
heaved a table into place,
but one leg rocked, and so she slid
a shim beneath to keep it still,
then brushed the top with a bundle of mint.
Here she set out Memeli olives,
cornelian cherries preserved in dregs,
endives, radishes, tulum cheese,
and hen eggs roasted in their shells,

all in earthenware; likewise
for wine a mixing bowl
of the same Sèvres, and cups carved
from beechwood sealed with yellow wax.
In no time, they ladled stew
steaming from the hearth and poured
a table wine of no great vintage,
and then they cleared for the final course
of nuts, dried figs, and shriveled dates,
and in a flat basket, apples
redolent of mellow sap
with a plump bunch of purple grapes.
In the center shone a honeycomb,
and above all shone those two sweet faces,
founts of endless care and kindness.
While everybody drained their cups,
the mixing bowl kept filling up
spontaneously, as if spring-fed,
and the couple saw the level rise.
Astonished by this miracle,
they clasped their trembling hands to pray
forgiveness for a sacred feast
they'd undertaken unawares.
They had but one goose—keeping watch
on the little farm as would a dog—

which the hosts resolved to catch
and serve the gods their guests.
It flapped around just out of reach,
eluding every feeble lunge
until the couple caught their breaths
as the goose seemed to run behind
the gods themselves for mercy,
who then with palms upraised
forbade that it be killed.
We're gods, they said. *This wicked town*
will pay what's due, with you alone
exempt from harm. Now leave your home
and follow up the mountain trail.
They both obeyed and set their sticks
against the rising slope.
When they reached the mountaintop,
the distance of an arrow shot,
they turned their eyes back and surveyed
a landscape sunk in swamp,
with only their one hut remaining.
While they wondered and while they wept
over their neighbors' fates,
their old house, snug for only two,
transformed into a temple:
forked posts swelled to columns,

thatch glittered as though gilded,
doors hardened into bronze
chased with friezes, and dirt floors
metamorphosed into marble.
Jove calmly spoke: *Good folk,*
deserving one another,
wish for anything you'd like.
They whispered awhile together,
and then Philemon revealed
to the holy ones their choice:
We wish to be your priests
and watch over your shrine.
And since we've shared such happy years,
let one hour take us both,
so I don't see her pyre
burn down to ash, nor she
dirt shoveled on my grave.
Granted: they would tend the place
for the time left, until released
from age into eternity.
One morning as they paused
before the temple steps,
talking of all that had occurred,
Philemon noticed Baucis
sprouting leaves, and Baucis Philemon:

stem and leaf, leaf and stem,

a crown sprang up above each face,

with only time to say goodbye,

goodbye and *all my love, my love,*

before the bark sealed shut their mouths.

Locals there still show the stranger

the trunks entwined from twin selves.

This story has the ring of truth,

told to me by elders

who had no cause to lie.

I've seen those branches hung with garlands,

and adding fresh ones, said:

May those who care for gods be gods,

and those who love be loved.

ANOTHER APRIL

A strange bird stood amid the flock,
doppelgänger of our Wyandotte,
but small, perhaps a bantam of the breed.
We called her April, for the month she came,
came and went with eerie ease,
escaping through the cyclone fence
as through a mirror,
more and more remote
with each egress,
her inscape of silver lace
so like the wire's woven links.

Three times I caught her in a landing net:
first high up in a tree,
then clucking through a private park,
where splatter from a fountain
embroidered hosta leaves,
and finally, on the yellow line
of Shenandoah Avenue,
scratching at a cricket
with the freedom of a jungle fowl.

Monofilaments of mesh
crushed her feet and feathers,
her haggard eye
almost aquiline in outrage.
Come what might, she would have lived
untrammeled, not this harried flight
from run and roost.
Neither tame nor wild,
with each declarative denial
she tangled further in the net
until I turned her loose.

THE LEASH

Bone idle, I gnaw the doorstop while I wait
for you to stir at last from sleeping late,
then with a clatter, boil a kettle, steep your tea,
and fog the kitchen window with humidity.
I tap the tiles and whine, *What of the day?*
You clear the cups and bowls, no more delay,
and from your enigmatic stream of talk,
my ear discerns the long-awaited *walk*.
You lock the door, and we resume the flow
of walking, going where we often go:
a left on Sidney Street, down Arkansas,
a few blocks to the park, and on through Shaw.
Though free, we take our customary route,
no end in mind except to walk about,
to sniff the wind, to see what we shall see;
a mobile state of mild expectancy.
Here we find a cage of seed and suet
suspended from a branch, and here a bluet
in bloom beside a pale blue plaster Mary.
I'm on the road, I got no time to tarry.

When firecracker dogs explode behind a fence
and chafe at each anomaly that gives offense,
my breath begins to rasp and hackles rise;
I strain against the leash and roll my eyes.
But even as I growl and grow more wild,
at every lunge I hear you calling, *Child!*
Edie, watch me! Then softer, *Don't be rude!*
My frenzy fades, my temperament subdued.
Shorn for spring, I'm hailed as muttonhead,
alpaca, goat, or any quadruped
that's raised for wool. *Who made thee, Little Lamb?*
I'm named for everything but what I am.
This morning, all things bark—pneumatic brakes, a sneeze—
no sentiments unsung in Tang anthologies.
A white-throated sparrow draws out its sour whistle,
as if to answer, *Here!* before the day's dismissal,
the unrecorded present, a flicker at the edge
of consciousness, above the privet hedge.
But humans live in absence, their thought and speech
adapted to abstractions out of reach.
In hats and coats, they paraphrase themselves
and hide in quotes of fruit and flower smells.
Trotting in a neighbor's wake, I sniff the sea,
a blend of oakmoss, ambergris, and celery,
and then a final breath of salt, tobacco, hay,

and something animal, before it fades away.
In masquerade—a dab of Shalimar—
they smell of anything but what they are.
Beside the school, I chase a rubber Kong,
a fetch of forty yards I run headlong,
rehearsing freedom with each outward bound
and deference each time I turn around
to custom, habit, power—constancies
of my regard for you, and yours for me.
Each liberty entails a bond of tenderness,
each sweet endearment comes with leash and harness:
obey, from *obaudire*, to hear and understand,
submitting to a click or syllable's command.
With thoughts of lunch, with thoughts of rich repast,
we swing through Compton Heights and saunter past
a block of cats, a colony of strays;
they flick their tails and I avert my gaze.
One sits atop a brick retaining wall
and with vast self-regard he surveys all
that passes by, but will not condescend
to rub against the fingers you extend.
Beside the curb, I root through trash and find
a spicy broth of smells to feed the mind.
Leave it, stubborn mule! I plant my feet
and hesitate, but soon admit defeat.

Good Eatie, Miss MacGreedy. Good E.T.!
What shall I do with this absurdity?
My fringe and ears recall a legal wig
that rides atop a spinning whirligig,
a brain that circles round and round the same
two syllables that form my human name.
When we have closed our circuit, home once more,
we climb the stairs, and you unlock the door,
admitting light to pierce the mellow gloom.
The smell of frying onions fills the room
from some ad hoc ragout or casserole,
while I make do with kibble in my bowl.
By afternoon, we go our separate ways.
You sit at desk and fret a battered phrase
or nose through dictionaries, on the scent
of obsolescent words and what they've meant.
Stock-still, you stare until the symbols signify,
as when a border collie gives her flock the eye,
while I curl on the couch, my breathing slow,
my thoughts unleashed to go where they will go.
Through inner dark, anonymous and free,
I dream that I am you, and you are me.

AT FIFTY: A LETTER

On Saturday morning, feeling fit,
I set out on a five-mile race
that starts and ends at Grace Court.
Summer has not yet relented,
here in mid-September,
but I found my rhythm easily,
moving downhill without pressure
through shadows, over fallen leaves,
among the breathing runners.
When I hit the three-mile mark
at the bottom of Old Salem,
my stopwatch read 22:10.
The course then climbed a long hill
on the new strollway beside Main;
then down, and up again
on First Street by the Rainbow
and Modern Chevrolet.
There I walked for ten seconds.
Redacted, blank, an interval
of who knows what duration . . .

I found myself sitting on a curb
trying hard not to pass out,
a fuzz of static in my brain.
As runners strode by, hands on hips,
I realized I was past the finish
clutching a small stick
with a very large number on it.

Police appeared with a cup of ice
and only left on my insistence
I felt better. But then the sun
came out from behind a cloud
and I worried that I couldn't move
myself into the shade.
With a wave, I stopped a passerby
and asked for a hand, my speech slurred.
She guided me to an open hydrant
where I could cool my head.
Eventually I got to my feet
and tottered home, recovered some,
went to the mountain, and took a nap.
When I awoke, I remembered crossing
the finish line, but without strength
to walk through the chute and take my stick.
I glimpsed someone in front of me

I took to be your uncle Dave,
unlikely as that sounds:
the same long energetic stride,
the same shaved neck and slight stoop.
When I tried to call him, I said *Dev!*
while realizing it wasn't you,
and so corrected myself to *Dave!*
Walking away, he turned to his friend
and muttered, *He seems a bit confused.*
I must have stood stock-still for minutes
before I staggered through the crowd.

It was like a stroke, but heatstroke
from not pausing at the water stops.
Remembering my foolishness
at the curb, as you might touch
a bruise to test its tenderness,
I sank into depression.
As usual, this spread
to every level of my life
for ten minutes, then I pushed back
from such thoughts. I'm fine now.

I hope you are enjoying school
and working through the *Odyssey*

with all its detours and digressions.
I'd rather you be there
(dozing in your carrel
behind a palisade of books)
than helping me through the gate.

AT NINETY-TWO

The worst will surely happen.
A killer in the dark,
a zombie's stiff rapacious lunge,
the swarm of insect appetite
that turns the lounge TV
to mothlight
could be no worse than this
assisted living,
the slow separation
of mind from all its objects,
never to touch the grass again,
sharp wit reduced
to dull amazement.
Whoever holds life dear
will find it soon devalued,
its food bereft of taste,
its doors decorated
like those of dorm rooms
by nephews or nurses
with arthritic handicrafts

you would have once disdained.
Staring at a dish
that surfaced in your hand,
your memory returns
to persimmons picked
after the first frost
and how they glowed
in the tin pail;
for a few days,
more than enough.

A TOAST

after Horace

Don't ask, we're not allowed to know
what end will come or when we'll go,
the end of us, of you and me
together, or each separately.
Genetics, habit, accident—
don't ask, and try to be content
to let the whitecaps do their worst
on this December thirty-first.
Let's raise a glass and shout *l'chaim*
above the squandered waves of time
that founder all our far-fetched schemes.
As we drift in talk, it seems
another year has slipped away
with nothing certain but today.

FUTILITIES

Enough rain
and every route
becomes an obstacle,

tracks turn to creeks,
roads to rivers,
the paths impassable.

*

From a neighbor's yard
the dull thud of walnuts,
the dead sound of digging,
an adult male voice
amused and scornful.

*

Almost done!
Almost done!
You're always

almost done,
which means
you're never
done with this,
with this,
the only ever
conversation.

*

She waited all afternoon and evening
until in bed at last she spoke
her mind, as if to drop a coin
a long way down, and through the dark
by way of answer to her thought
came only the sound of breathing.

*

By force of habit
you inhabit
the site of love,

nothing left
beyond a slight
depression in a field.

*

The scrawled inscription
on a square of sidewalk reads
Sadie and John forever;
they both still live nearby.

*

Has anyone, in thirty years,
tried the door to find it locked?

PRUFROCK

The sun goes down in pallid flames
behind flat roofs and chimney pots
and through the slits of gangways,
to blaze with cold lasciviousness
across a window's streaky surface.
It lights the sheet on which I scratch
scenes from a receding past—
interior, a whitewashed room,
inverted cameos in spoons—
and when the page grows dim, I watch
a shadow flood the melon patch.

Across the alley, they resume
their argument, an old routine:
from deep within the house, unseen,
she rants and raves. What has he done?
And why does he remain so calm?
Locked out and leaning on
the back door, he taps the glass
and mutters, *Val, please let me in,*
then louder, taps the glass again.

I happen to know, that very house—
like every house along the block,
built of red brick in the aughts—
belonged to one Carl Wilhelm Prufrock,
a Brandenburg-born *Hersteller*
of fine household sofas and chairs,
bluff, yet flustered by his heirs
as by upholsterers on strike.
Why not rest, at sixty-one?
He left the thriving enterprise
to Harry, *ein guter Sohn*,
bustling, gregarious,
and never at a loss for words:
A clean sweep in parlor goods!
J. Alfred seems to have received
no mention in his father's will
and no place in the company.
The lad was, after all, quite frail,
fastidious, and often curled
all morning on a blue settee
in his imaginary world.
He sat so still, his spindly frame
mingled with the furniture
until he all but disappeared,
awaiting a knock that never came.
I understand the letter J

stood for the generic John,
befitting anonymity;
he left not so much as a stone.
His family lies in Bellefontaine,
upholstered caskets sunk beneath
sculpted marble urn and wreath.
Well, the house is much the same.

The sun has set; the shouting stopped,
and with a click the door unlocked.
Upstairs, a pale blue light turns on,
some new stage in the long debate,
intensities of love or hate
reduced to shadows, curtains drawn.

LIVING DEAD

Those days, when I was dealing,
I had no time for them.
I missed my oldest walking
across the high-school gym
while I waited for my self-disgust
to shuffle down the block
like Lazarus in a cloud of dust.
Now what's the use of talk?
Come home, they say, each time they call.

Am I the kind of mother
that you call *good enough*?
My son's become a stranger,
his manner cool and tough.
My little girl has just turned nine
and more than anything
I want to give her back the time
we lost at sentencing.
Come home, they say, each time they call.

My kids, they love *The Walking Dead*.
By some calamity,
a zombie pathogen has spread
through all humanity,
and as the flesh disintegrates
a sheriff's officer
walks across the Southern States
to try and find a cure.
Come home, they say, each time they call.

I'm not that into it, but still,
I'm learning all I can
and slogging through the months until
my life begins again
among my old belongings,
as rattled keys recall
the turbulence and longings
of this dark interval.
Come home, they say, each time they call.
Come home soon or not at all.

BEULAH LAND

Going home means anywhere
but here, putting aside
worn grays
for the bright amber
of a fall morning.
No more counting days
in the clack and steam of laundry.

With the hush of brakes
a Greyhound bus
glides beneath the trees
and past a shuttered smelter.
Grisaille shadows.
Chains of geese.
A swath of sheepish sunlight

on foothills south of Zion.
As day dims
the windows turn
to mirrors

and the coach hums
with quiet conversation,
murmurs into cell phones.

How might freedom feel
after seven years away?
Vibrations through
the bootheel,
with a cardboard box
and bus fare
to any place but here.

LINGERING IN ALABAMA

We take cold consolation
   from smoke through winter trees
and cotton blowing through the grass
   like snowflakes on the seas.

We draw a thimbleful of warmth
   from the little daylight left
to flit through Sipsey woods where shadows
   weave a shuttled weft.

Belated whistles pierce the chill,
   a note of happiness
the wind has whittled down to wit,
   sharp and comfortless.

We find scant reassurance
   where no blaze marks the trail
and the ruckus of cowcumber leaves
   has left a shredded sail.

Like an ocean liner's rusted hull
　　arrested on its course,
the scarp face looms above a canyon
　　shaped by shapeless force.

We take cold consolation
　　in *whoit wit wit wit,*
the sound of water dripping from
　　the branch on which we sit.

What islands, at what distances,
　　disperse beneath the skies?
You've stayed too long, you've stayed too long!
　　the setting sun replies.

LITTLE EGYPT

Counterclockwise
a vulture circles
the point of emptiness

rising above a rotting corpse
once a deer
diluted with distance
until it smells of musk

while at the foot
of a river bluff
in underbrush
a brown thrasher
gets on with the work
of flipping hickory hulls
for the flutter of insect life

as a solicitor fossicks
among old files
in uncontested solitude

the long sifting
of a legal process

drop it drop it
pick it up
pick it up
cover it up

stet

stet

CHESTER, ILLINOIS

Cloud piles on cloud; keel scrapes sand.
Coal dust drifts from a rusty barge,
the river full of silt, field soldered to field,
even the light heavy. Far from the sea
Popeye reels along a gravel road
with an oar against his shoulder.
On Swanwick Street, the rare tourist
en route to somewhere else
ruminates on myths displaced.
Rough House cooks an omelet
as patrons trade in cattle futures.
The first stirrings before a storm
stroke the wings of the Whiffle Hen
drooping in sleep on a porch rail
as scrapings of "Harvest Home" drift down
from windows of the opera house
in flurries of rosin. Far from the sea,
far from its whip and precipitous glare,
a floodplain streaked with rills
condenses the leaden light.

Travelers from vast spaces
or truckers in a turnout
check their instruments
and test infinitives
against each hole and hollow:
to spend the day in a rain barrel,
to scour the kitchen clean,
to curl beneath an olive quilt,
an ember under ash.

BIÈRE DE GARDE

How good it is, to sip a beer
outdoors, with winter drawing near,
above the wreckage of a meal.

How good, before the bill comes due,
to watch a copper light gleam through
an ale infused with chanterelle

and trust yourself to only those
sensations of the tongue and nose,
what's felt, and how it makes you feel.

A sip held in the mouth evokes
a golden bloom among the oaks
and water drawn up from a well

one afternoon spent near the source
of happiness, atop a horse
that now stands idle in its stall.

These days you keep too much inside,
but once you foraged far and wide
through pastures north of Carbondale.

How fine, that you have faintly caught
a sour note of apricot
so deep in the cloudy dregs of fall,

the past in what has come to pass,
and cradle in your palm a glass
of *once*, a final swig of ale.

NOTES FROM A CAMPAIGN

They set up in the yard, in dappled shade,
a light breeze, their maps and books arrayed
on tabletops, with dice for paperweights.
But characters float free from all constraints:
in single file, they wind like a slow air
through Browning Pass and down the Broken Stair,
Sophia's dwarf in front to clear the snow,
and then the gnome, a string of mules in tow,
and finally, the young transgender elf,
a druid with the skill to change herself
into a lynx or fox or bird of prey.
After all, they gather here to play
a game that could admit of anything
the mind admits—a spell of summoning
that floats an eagle through the evening sky,
a blade that flashes with a tumbling die,
or slick reptilian scales that catch the sun;
perhaps no better world than ours, but one
in which disasters bring hilarity
and every danger holds some novelty.
While daylight lasts, they laugh and talk amidst

a world that would not otherwise exist.
All winter long, they had been trapped inside
their separate homes, their minds preoccupied.
They watched the snowfall turn to steady rain,
and with the spring, resumed their long campaign.
Down a mountain spur and through a deep
ravine, the company draws near a keep:
serrated battlements shred the strands
of frozen fog that float across these lands.
Through fog, there looms an ogre standing guard
encased in ice, his body frozen hard,
his face contracted in a wince of pain,
while further on, the dragon Cryovain
has curled in sleep around the kitchen roof,
each breath a polar blast and living proof
that such archaic forces still hold sway
and hoard unspoken secrets, hid away
yet held in mind, antiques that crowd the earth
beneath their feet. What risk are such things worth?
Why not escape to Neverwinter Wood
or ride at ease along the ocean road?
Because the players want a darker thrill,
the druid chants and scatters dust until
an anvil thunderhead begins to mass
and folding chairs sit empty on the grass.

KUDZU

Waves rise. Heaps without horizon
heave across a mountainside,
overwhelming works of cast-iron whimsy,
what might be trees rendered as mass,
every line overgrown,
planes of leaf detached from props
to float on furry stems.

Do catbirds flit beneath the canopy?
Does an old woman still stoop
over the potato she peels
in quiet concentration?
We've lived beneath these leaves so long
complaints become traditional.
Twined with trumpet vine and muscadine
in arabesques unending,
kudzu has camouflaged
a patch of Yadkin County
in abstract calligraphy,
a topographic map
without culture or legend.

However you handle form,
leave no fingerprints.
When you stir ink,
your brushstrokes have already dried.
From the moment you grasp a brush,
sit idle, doing nothing.

Syntax loosened, laces untied,
kudzu masters a bridge
with flying buttresses
as the river below
relaxes into a bend,
even the names—
Yatkin, Reatkin, Sapona—sunk
in deep and wild obscurity.
Sit here long enough, you'll see
a tendril creep toward sunlight
and time fan into space.

A BAT IN DAYLIGHT

Along the bluffs in early spring
as you were riding piggyback
you hollered, *Wait! I saw something*
in an evergreen beside the trail,
an ornament of orange and black,
a fuzzy pear with triangles.
We stopped and wandered back a bit.
Then I too saw the ginger thing—
unnameable but definite,
bewitched and altogether weird—
until it stretched inverted wings,
untucked its head, and disappeared.

COLD TRAIL

The feeling of time derives from heat,
an agitation of molecules,
oracles from the friction of air
through fissures and the leaves of oaks.
A few gnats stitch the lake's edge
where a fox turns off the gravel road
to nose through rhododendron
as children crawl through winter coats
to reach a closet's dark recess.
Dawdling at the edge of sleep
you work through problems already past
though unresolved, a notional path,
a crease through heads of wild blue phlox
that waking, you can't follow.

FIFTEEN

She cuts across an open space,
a field where she played many matches,
intensities that don't leave much
to memory, those pitched battles
as in fields around Manassas,
woods and fields around Manassas:
these things took place and left a place,
a public dream now only grass,
the smell, nostalgia's commonplace
of green-leaf volatiles in flux
and irreversibly dispersed
(according to her physics class)
through random thermal motion, first
a mower's drone, and then a breeze
to stir the grass and distant trees.

TRIBUTARY

Down one road or another, beyond a bridge abutment,
an iron plaque commemorates the USS *Neosho*,
a Cimarron-class oiler, Cimarron from *Río
de los Carneros Cimarrón*, river of the wild sheep
that runs through Oklahoma. Pump jacks nod in the distance
somewhere south of Tulsa, the crude oil light and sweet,
reservoirs that filled a tanker launched in 1939
and hit by Zeros three years later in the Coral Sea,
set ablaze and listing in ocean depth so crystalline
it seemed another troposphere, a thickening of air
that buoyed the ship. A slick extended from its hull
for nights and days until a destroyer
arrived to save the crew and scuttle the *Neosho*,

which took its name from this little river
so far from any ocean, Osage for clear, cold water.

LANDFALL

NEW ZEALAND

Te Piha with its stone prow
carves a wake in the Tasman Sea,
the last known ship from Scheria
(Book 13 of the *Odyssey*),
swift as a skua on the wind,
now sunk in black volcanic sand.
Above the beach, a wooden bach
rattles with rain on its tin roof
like sticks on a tumutumu.
The wind, though silent against itself,
scrapes against whatever boughs
have bent or broken. Even now
a lone surfer paddles through
the storm's radiating shocks,
then turns and rises to his feet,
hesitates, and takes the drop
on a long left-hand break, its curl
the spirula of a ram's horn shell.

His board, with the sound of ripping cloth,

chatters against the surface chop

as the wave collapses into froth

and then transparent sheets that slide

one across another,

always never quite arrived.

KEA

A circus of kea encircles the van,
each parrot an olive-green Pierrot,
an artichoke fluffed against the chill.
They circle around an olive sedan,
whistle and croak, scrape and bow,
but given half a chance they will
uproot your antenna mast and rip
the weather stripping from your cowl,
just as they rip apart a sheep
for suet—nothing personal.
Their cry *keeeaaa* declares *I am*,
but what? Sheer curiosity,
the mind a scheme, a diagram
of hunger's hidden circuitry.

TUI

Te tu e hu! Te tu e hu!

MAORI SONG

This bird does not refer to you,
not understood but overheard.
Watchful behind its repertoire,
it sings from kōtukutuku
of flow and friction, undeterred
by those who listen from afar
or stand beneath the shedding tree.
Tui does not derive from *tu*
but occupies the echoed song
of *kō-ka-ko* and *pī-pi-pi*,
each bird a name, each name a tune
to whistle as you walk along
preoccupied with the rise and fall
of each reflexive, raucous call.

THE MARLBOROUGH SOUNDS

Aboard the Interislander
as if inside a bronze bell
a low drone vibrates the hull,
hold full of parked cars,
twenty thousand tons afloat.
What old weight of feeling
has settled in your bones?

A hammer clangs somewhere
beneath the waterline,
a prolonged reverberation
rich in overtones,
pulling a deep draft
through sea-drowned valleys.

Up top, cold wind whips
your camera strap against the rail,
a foil's flick, hankering to find
a cap to roll along the deck,
weightless and uncontainable,
with joy a flame to flutter.

A mollymawk sits on a swell
before the bow and glances back
from beneath a black brow
in time to take off—
blades of wings stiffly extended,
feet patting the tops of waves
as if a shallow puddle.

ACKNOWLEDGMENTS

These poems previously appeared in *Kenyon Review, Liberties, The New Criterion, The News Station, PN Review, Poetry, Subtropics,* and *ZAZA*.

"Monody" adapts a line from James Henry's poem "Another and another and another." Georgia Blizzard (1919–2002) was a ceramic artist from Virginia. In "The First Troubadour," "Then looke who list" is a passing phrase from Edmund Spenser's "An Hymne of Heavenly Beautie." In "New France," *"les nuages qui passent"* is a quote from Charles Baudelaire's "L'étranger." "The Leash" alludes to poems by George Herbert, among others. In "Lingering in Alabama," the bird-song is that of a yellow-breasted chat. "Chester, Illinois" translates a line from Jean Follain's poem "Signes pour voyageurs." In "Bière de Garde," thanks go to Scratch Brewing in Ava, Illinois, for the chanterelle bière de garde.

Thanks also to Jeff Clark, Jonathan Galassi, Michael O'Leary, and Peter O'Leary for their help and encouragement.